Macaroni & Cheese

by Christina Leaf

BLASTOFF!
3
READERS

BELLWETHER MEDIA • MINNEAPOLIS, MN

Note to Librarians, Teachers, and Parents:

Blastoff! Readers are carefully developed by literacy experts and combine standards-based content with developmentally appropriate text.

Level 1 provides the most support through repetition of high-frequency words, light text, predictable sentence patterns, and strong visual support.

Level 2 offers early readers a bit more challenge through varied simple sentences, increased text load, and less repetition of high-frequency words.

Level 3 advances early-fluent readers toward fluency through increased text and concept load, less reliance on visuals, longer sentences, and more literary language.

Level 4 builds reading stamina by providing more text per page, increased use of punctuation, greater variation in sentence patterns, and increasingly challenging vocabulary.

Level 5 encourages children to move from "learning to read" to "reading to learn" by providing even more text, varied writing styles, and less familiar topics.

Whichever book is right for your reader, Blastoff! Readers are the perfect books to build confidence and encourage a love of reading that will last a lifetime!

This edition first published in 2020 by Bellwether Media, Inc.

No part of this publication may be reproduced in whole or in part without written permission of the publisher. For information regarding permission, write to Bellwether Media, Inc., Attention: Permissions Department, 6012 Blue Circle Drive, Minnetonka, MN 55343.

Library of Congress Cataloging-in-Publication Data

Names: Leaf, Christina, author.
Title: Macaroni & Cheese / by Christina Leaf.
Other titles: Macaroni and cheese
Description: Minneapolis, MN : Bellwether Media, Inc., 2020. | Series: Blastoff! readers. Our favorite foods |
   Includes bibliographical references and index. | Audience: Ages 5-8. | Audience: Grades 2-3. |
   Summary: "Simple text and full-color photography introduce beginning readers to macaroni & cheese.
Developed by literacy experts for students in kindergarten through third grade"-- Provided by publisher.
Identifiers: LCCN 2019026667 (print) | LCCN 2019026668 (ebook) | ISBN 9781644871461 (library binding) |
   ISBN 9781618918222 (ebook)
Subjects: LCSH: Cooking (Pasta)--Juvenile literature. | Cooking (Cheese)--Juvenile literature. | Convenience foods-
   -Juvenile literature. | LCGFT: Cookbooks.
Classification: LCC TX809.M17 L43 2020 (print) | LCC TX809.M17 (ebook) | DDC 641.82/2--dc23
LC record available at https://lccn.loc.gov/2019026667
LC ebook record available at https://lccn.loc.gov/2019026668

Editor: Kate Moening   Designer: Jeffrey Kollock

Printed in the United States of America, North Mankato, MN.

Table of Contents

Comfort Food

School was hard today. But your dad serves warm macaroni and cheese for dinner. Instant comfort!

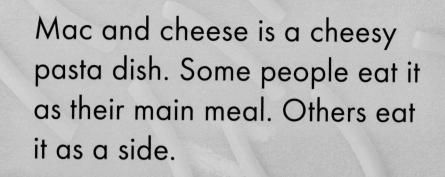

Mac and cheese is a cheesy pasta dish. Some people eat it as their main meal. Others eat it as a side.

Macaroni and cheese is made with pasta, cheese, and butter.

How to Make Macaroni & Cheese

1 Cook pasta

2 Prepare cheese sauce

3 Combine and bake in oven

macaroni & cheese
ingredients

People may make it on the stove from a box. Others use fresh **ingredients**. They can bake it in an oven.

Macaroni & Cheese History

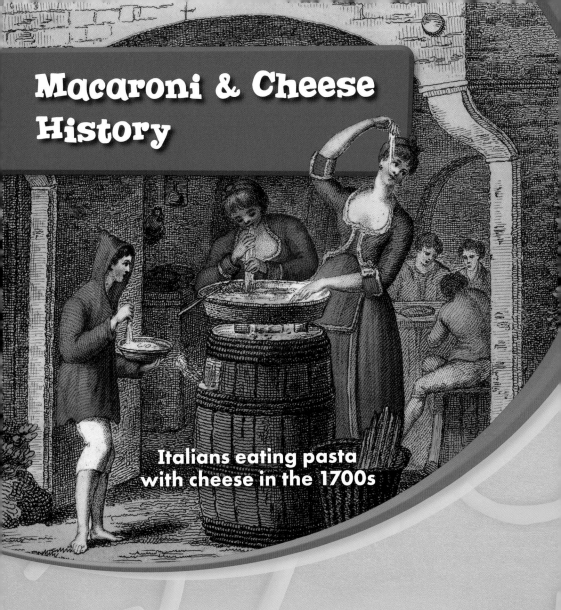

Italians eating pasta
with cheese in the 1700s

Macaroni and cheese has an
uncertain beginning. Many
researchers think pasta with
cheese first appeared in Naples,
Italy, during the **Middle Ages**.

8

But a more modern **recipe** came in the 1400s from Switzerland. It included butter and cream.

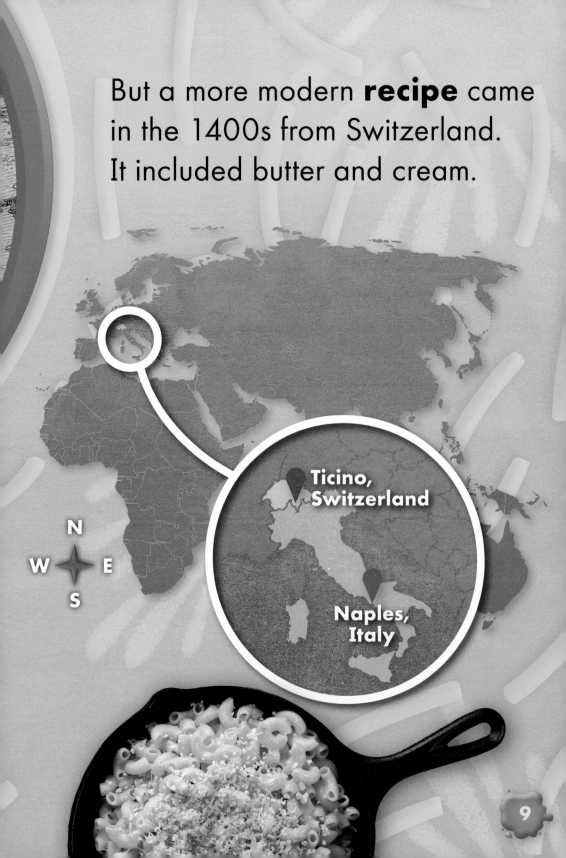

Ticino, Switzerland

Naples, Italy

N
W E
S

Mac and cheese was first recorded in the United States in 1802. President Thomas Jefferson served it at a **state dinner**.

Thomas Jefferson

Only the rich ate the dish.
Macaroni was costly.

Macaroni became cheaper in the late 1800s.

Macaroni & Cheese Timeline

1400s

Maestro Martino includes a recipe for Sicilian macaroni in his cookbook

1824

An American cookbook features a recipe for macaroni and cheese

1937

Kraft introduces boxed mac and cheese

southern
comfort food

Freed **slaves** who once cooked mac and cheese for the rich made it for their own families. This made it a **staple** of southern U.S. kitchens.

13

Simple Mac & Cheese

Have an adult help you make this tasty mac and cheese!

Ingredients

- 1 1/2 cups milk
- 1 teaspoon black pepper
- 1 cup shredded cheddar cheese
- 1 teaspoon salt
- 1/4 tablespoon dry mustard

- 1 tablespoon flour
- 1 small onion, diced
- 2 tablespoons of butter
- 1 package elbow macaroni or other short noodles

Instructions

1. In a large saucepan, cook noodles as directed and drain.
2. Preheat oven to 350 degrees Fahrenheit (177 degrees Celsius).
3. Grease the casserole or baking dish.
4. In another saucepan, add butter and onion. Cook until onion is soft.
5. Add flour, mustard, salt, and pepper. Stir.
6. Stir in milk. Continue stirring until the mixture has thickened.
7. Remove from heat and stir in cheese to create a sauce.
8. Spoon macaroni into the baking dish. Pour the sauce over the noodles.
9. Bake until bubbly and golden, about 20 minutes. Let cool.

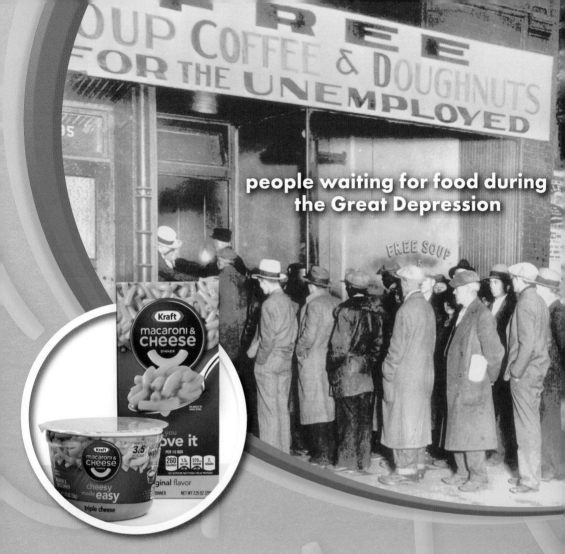

people waiting for food during the Great Depression

The dish grew more popular during the **Great Depression**. In 1937, Kraft introduced boxed mac and cheese. Struggling families could afford this cheap meal. Wartime **rations** made it even more common.

Macaroni & Cheese Today

lobster
mac & cheese

barbecue
mac & cheese

Mac and cheese is a much-loved dish today! People **vary** the pasta and cheeses used.

People also add items like hot dogs or broccoli. Some top their pasta with bread crumbs or barbecue sauce!

Popular Macaroni Noodles

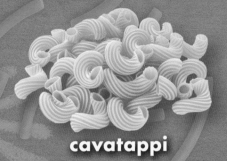
cavatappi

elbows

radiatore

rigatoni

rotini

shells

Macaroni and cheese takes many forms. In the southern U.S., the dish is thick and gooey. It is creamier in the north. The noodles might top pizza or burgers. Deep-fried mac and cheese bites are popular snacks!

mac & cheese burger

deep-fried
mac & cheese bites

Grilled Mac & Cheese Sandwiches

Have an adult help you with this cheesy dish!

Tools

- spatula
- griddle or frying pan

Ingredients

- bread
- 1 tablespoon butter
- 1-2 slices cheddar cheese
- 4 slices bacon
- leftover macaroni and cheese

Instructions

1. Heat pan on medium heat. Use half of the butter to grease the pan, then put one slice of bread in the pan.

2. Place cheese, bacon, and mac and cheese on top of the bread. Put the other slice of bread on top.

3. When the bottom bread is golden (about 4-5 minutes), lift the sandwich with the spatula.

4. Add the rest of the butter to grease the pan.

5. Carefully flip the sandwich and cook until the other side is golden.

Some recipes make mac and cheese healthier. Zucchini noodles are a popular **substitute**. Kraft added cauliflower to some of its boxed pastas.

These tasty changes keep the cheesy dish popular!

cauliflower
mac & cheese

making zucchini
noodles

Glossary

Great Depression—a period of time from the late 1920s through the 1930s when people did not have a lot of money

ingredients—items that make up a food

Middle Ages—a period of European history from about 500 to 1500

rations—the amount of food allowed by the government; foods like cheese and milk were rationed during World War II so there would be enough to feed soldiers.

recipe—a set of instructions for making a specific food

slaves—people who are treated like property; African Americans were bought and sold as slaves in the Southern United States until the late 1800s.

staple—a widely used food or other item

state dinner—a fancy meal hosted by the president or another government leader when other country leaders are visiting

substitute—something that is used in place of something else

vary—to change or make different

To Learn More

AT THE LIBRARY

Green, Sara. *Kraft*. Minneapolis, Minn.: Bellwether Media, 2017.

Heos, Bridget. *From Milk to Cheese*. Mankato, Minn.: Amicus, 2018.

Rajczak, Kristen. *Perfect Pasta Recipes*. New York, N.Y.: Gareth Stevens Publishing, 2015.

ON THE WEB

FACTSURFER

Factsurfer.com gives you a safe, fun way to find more information.

1. Go to www.factsurfer.com.

2. Enter "macaroni & cheese" into the search box and click 🔍.

3. Select your book cover to see a list of related web sites.

Index